G

Published by Windmill Books, Inc.
257 Park Avenue South
New York, New York 10010

First Printing

ISBN 0-87807-015-X Trade
Library of Congress Catalog Card Number 71-148174
Manufactured in Japan

THE LORD IS MY SHEPHERD

PICTURES BY
GEORGE KRAUS

Windmill Books

TO MY DAUGHTERS
BEATRICE AND DIANE.

THE LORD IS MY

SHEPHERD

I SHALL NOT WANT

HE MAKETH ME TO LIE DOWN

IN GREEN PASTURES.

HE LEADETH ME
BESIDE THE STILL WATERS.

HE RESTORETH
MY SOUL :

HE LEADETH ME IN THE PATHS
OF RIGHTEOUSNESS
FOR HIS NAME'S SAKE.

YEA, THOUGH I WALK
THROUGH THE VALLEY
OF THE SHADOW OF DEATH
I WILL FEAR NO EVIL;
FOR THOU ART WITH ME.

THY ROD AND THY STAFF
THEY COMFORT ME.

THOU PREPAREST A TABLE
BEFORE ME IN THE
PRESENCE OF MINE
ENEMIES.

THOU ANOINTEST
MY HEAD WITH OIL,
MY CUP RUNNETH OVER

SURELY GOODNESS
AND MERCY
SHALL FOLLOW ME
ALL THE DAYS
OF MY LIFE:

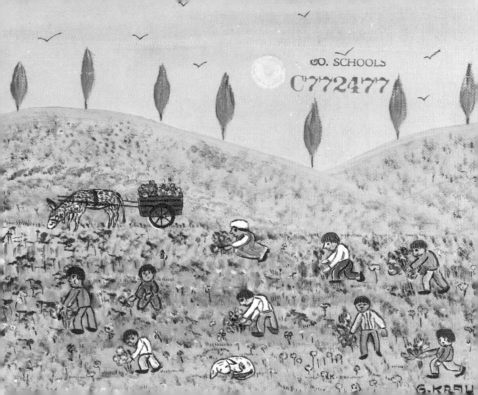

AND I WILL DWELL

IN THE HOUSE OF THE LORD

G. KRAUS

GEORGE KRAUS